plays

To Gerry, a frightening
play for a happy
halloween

Lancelot

11-93

by the same author

*

THE MAIDS

A Play

by

JEAN GENET

translated
from the French by
BERNARD FRECHTMAN

faber and faber

First published in England in 1957
by Faber and Faber Limited
3 Queen Square, London WC1
First published in this edition 1963
Reprinted 1965, 1970, 1974, 1978 and 1983
Printed in Great Britain by
Whitstable Litho Ltd, Whitstable, Kent
All rights reserved

ISBN 0 571 05461 7

THE CHARACTERS

SOLANGE	⎰ Two housemaids, sisters, thirty to thirty-five
CLAIRE	⎱ years old. Solange is the elder.
MADAME	Their mistress. She is about twenty-five.

LES BONNES was first produced in this country in French in 1952 at the Mercury Theatre, Notting Hill Gate, under the auspices of the Institute of Contemporary Arts.

Cast

SOLANGE	Selma Vaz Dias
CLAIRE	Olive Gregg
MADAME	Oriel Ross
Decor by	Eduardo Paolozzi
Directed by	Peter Zadek

This production was transferred to the Royal Court Theatre for a short season.

Cast

SOLANGE	Selma Vaz Dias
CLAIRE	Olive Gregg
MADAME	Betty Stockfield
Decor by	David de Bethel
Directed by	Peter Zadek

The first production in English took place at the New Lindsey Theatre Club on 5th June 1956.

Cast

SOLANGE	Selma Vaz Dias
CLAIRE	Hazel Penwarden
MADAME	Betty Stockfield
Decor by	Nigel Whittaker
Directed by	Peter Zadek

Madame's bedroom. Louis-Quinze furniture. Lace. Rear, a window opening on the front of the house opposite. Right, a bed. Left, a door and a dressing table. Flowers in profusion. The time is evening.

(Claire, wearing a slip, is standing with her back to the dressing table. Her gestures—arm extended—and tone are exaggeratedly tragic.)

CLAIRE: Those gloves! Those eternal gloves! I've told you time and again to leave them in the kitchen. You probably hope to seduce the milkman with them. No, no, don't lie; that won't get you anywhere! Hang them over the sink. When *will* you understand that this room is not to be sullied. Everything, yes, everything that comes out of the kitchen is spit! So stop it! *(During this speech, Solange has been playing with a pair of rubber gloves and observing her gloved hands, which are alternately spread fanwise and folded in the form of a bouquet.)* Make yourself quite at home. Preen like a peacock. And above all, don't hurry, we've plenty of time. Go!
(Solange's posture changes and she leaves humbly, holding the rubber gloves with her fingertips. Claire sits down at the dressing table. She sniffs at the flowers, runs her hand over the toilet articles, brushes her hair, pats her face.)
Get my dress ready. Quick! Time presses. Are you there? *(She turns round.)* Claire! Claire!
(Solange enters.)
SOLANGE: I beg Madame's pardon, I was preparing her tea. *(She pronounces it "tay".)*
CLAIRE: Lay out my things. The white spangled dress. The fan. The emeralds.
SOLANGE: Very well, Madame. All Madame's jewels?
CLAIRE: Put them out and I shall choose. And, of course, my patent-leather slippers. The ones you've had your eye

7

on for years. (*Solange takes a few jewel boxes from the closet, opens them, and lays them out on the bed.*) For your wedding, no doubt. Admit he seduced you! Just look at you! How big you are! Admit it! (*Solange squats on the rug, spits on the patent-leather slippers, and polishes them.*) I've told you, Claire, with*out* spit. Let it sleep in you, my child, let it stagnate. Ah! Ah! (*She giggles nervously.*) May the lost wayfarer drown in it. Ah! Ah! You *are* hideous. Lean forward and look at yourself in my shoes. Do you think I find it pleasant to know that my foot is shrouded by the veils of your saliva? By the mists of your swamps?

SOLANGE: (*on her knees, and very humble.*) I wish Madame to be lovely.

CLAIRE: I shall be. (*She primps in front of the mirror.*) You hate me, don't you? You crush me with your attentions and your humbleness; you smother me with gladioli and mimosa. (*She stands up and, lowering her tone*) There are too many flowers. The room is needlessly cluttered. It's *impossible.* (*She looks at herself again in the glass.*) I shall be lovely. Lovelier than you'll ever be. With a face and body like that, you'll never seduce Mario.
(*Dropping the tragic tone*) A ridiculous young milkman despises us, and if we're going to have a kid by him——

SOLANGE: Oh! I've never——

CLAIRE: (*resuming*). Be quiet, you fool. My dress!

SOLANGE: (*she looks in the closet, pushing aside a few dresses*). The red dress. Madame will wear the red dress.

CLAIRE: I said the white dress, the one with spangles.

SOLANGE: (*firmly*). I'm sorry. Madame will wear the scarlet velvet dress this evening.

CLAIRE: (*naively*). Ah? Why?

SOLANGE: (*coldly*). It's impossible to forget Madame's bosom under the velvet folds. And the jet brooch, when Madame was sighing and telling Monsieur of my devotion! Your widowhood really requires that you be entirely in black.

CLAIRE: Eh?

8

SOLANGE: Need I say more? A word to the wise——

CLAIRE: Ah! So you want to talk. . . . Very well. Threaten me. Insult your mistress, Solange. You want to talk about Monsieur's misfortunes, don't you? Fool. It was hardly the moment to allude to him, but I can turn this matter to fine account! You're smiling? Do you doubt it?

SOLANGE: The time is not yet ripe to unearth——

CLAIRE: What a word! My infamy! My infamy! To unearth!

SOLANGE: Madame!

CLAIRE: Am I to be at your mercy for having denounced Monsieur to the police, for having sold him? And yet I'd have done even worse, or better. You think I haven't suffered? Claire, I forced my hand to pen the letter—without mistakes in spelling or syntax, without crossing anything out—the letter that sent my lover to prison. And you, instead of standing by me, you mock me. You force your colours on me! You speak of widowhood! He isn't dead. Claire, Monsieur will be led from prison to prison, perhaps even to Devil's Island, where I, his mistress, mad with grief, shall follow him. I shall be in the convoy. I shall share his glory. You speak of widowhood and deny me the white gown—the mourning of queens. You're unaware of that, Claire——

SOLANGE: (coldly). Madame will wear the red dress.

CLAIRE: (simply). Quite. (Severely.) Hand me the dress. Oh! I'm so alone and friendless. I can see in your eyes that you loathe me. You don't care what happens to me.

SOLANGE: I'll follow you everywhere. I love you.

CLAIRE: No doubt. As one loves a mistress. You love and respect me. And you're hoping for a legacy, a codicil in your favour——

SOLANGE: I'd do all in my power——

CLAIRE: (ironically). I know. You'd go through fire for me. (Solange helps Claire put on her dress.) Fasten it. Don't pull so hard. Don't try to bind me. (Solange kneels at Claire's feet and arranges the folds of the dress.) Avoid pawing me. You smell like an animal. You've brought

9

those odours from some foul attic, where the lackeys
visit us at night. The maid's room! The garret!
(*Graciously*) Claire, if I speak of the smell of garrets, it
is for memory's sake. And of the twin beds where two
sisters fall asleep, dreaming of one another. There,
(*she points to a spot in the room*) there, the two iron beds
with the night table between them. There, (*she points
to a spot opposite*) the pinewood dresser with the little
altar to the Holy Virgin! That's right, isn't it?

SOLANGE: We're so unhappy. I could cry! If you go on——

CLAIRE: It *is* right, isn't it! Let's skip the business of your
prayers and kneeling. I shan't even mention the paper
flowers. . . . (*She laughs.*) Paper flowers! And the branch
of holy boxwood! (*She points to the flowers in the room.*)
Just look at these flowers open in my honour! Claire,
am I not a lovelier Virgin?

SOLANGE: (*as if in adoration*). Be quiet——

CLAIRE: And there, (*she points to a very high spot at the window*)
that notorious skylight from which a half-naked
milkman jumps to your bed!

SOLANGE: Madame is forgetting herself, Madame——

CLAIRE: And what about your hands? Don't *you* forget your
hands. How often have I (*she hesitates*) murmured: they
befoul the sink.

SOLANGE: The fall!

CLAIRE: Eh?

SOLANGE: (*arranging the dress on Claire's hips*). The fall of your
dress. I'm arranging your fall from grace.

CLAIRE: Get away, you bungler! (*She kicks Solange in the temple
with her Louis-Quinze heel. Solange, who is kneeling,
staggers and draws back.*)

SOLANGE: Oh! Me a burglar?

CLAIRE: I said bungler; and if you must whimper, do it in your
garret. Here, in my bedroom, I will have only noble
tears. A time will come when the hem of my gown
will be studded with them, but those will be precious
tears. Arrange my train, you clod.

SOLANGE: (*in ecstasy*). Madame's being carried away!

CLAIRE: By the devil! He's carrying me away in his fragrant arms. He's lifting me up, I leave the ground, I'm off. . . . (*She stamps with her heel.*) And I stay behind. Get my necklace! But hurry, we won't have time. If the gown's too long, make a hem with some safety pins. (*Solange gets up and goes to take the necklace from a jewel case, but Claire rushes ahead of her and seizes the jewels. Her fingers graze those of Solange, and she recoils in horror.*) Keep your hands off mine! I can't stand your touching me. Hurry up!

SOLANGE: There's no need to overdo it. Your eyes are ablaze.

CLAIRE: (*shocked astonishment*). What's that you said?

SOLANGE: Limits, boundaries, Madame. Frontiers are not conventions but laws. Here, my lands; there, your shore——

CLAIRE: What language, my dear. Claire, do you mean that I've already crossed the seas? Are you offering me the dreary exile of your imagination? You're taking revenge, aren't you? You feel the time coming when, no longer a maid——

SOLANGE: You see straight through me. You divine my thoughts.

CLAIRE: (*increasingly carried away*)—the time coming when, no longer a maid, you become vengeance itself, but, Claire, don't forget—Claire, are you listening?—don't forget, it was the maid who hatched schemes of vengeance, and I—Claire, you're not listening.

SOLANGE: (*absent-mindedly*). I'm listening.

CLAIRE: And I contain within me both vengeance and the maid and give them a chance for life, a chance for salvation. Claire, it's a burden, it's terribly painful to be a mistress, to contain all the springs of hatred, to be the dunghill on which you grow. You want to see me naked every day. I *am* beautiful, am I not? And the desperation of my love makes me even more so, but you have no idea what strength I need!

SOLANGE: (*contemptuously*). Your lover!

CLAIRE: My unhappy lover heightens my nobility. Yes. Yes, my child. All that you'll ever know is your own baseness.

SOLANGE: That'll do! Now hurry! Are you ready?

CLAIRE: Are you?

SOLANGE: (*she steps back to the wardrobe*). I'm ready.—I'm tired of being an object of disgust. I hate you, too. I despise you. I hate your scented bosom. Your . . . *ivory* bosom! Your . . . *golden* thighs! Your . . . *amber* feet! I hate you! (*She spits on the red dress.*)

CLAIRE: (*aghast*). Oh! . . . Oh! . . . But. . . .

SOLANGE: (*walking up to her*). Yes, my proud beauty. You think you can always do just as you like. You think you can deprive me forever of the beauty of the sky, that you can choose your perfumes and powders, your nail-polish and silk and velvet and lace, and deprive *me* of them? That you can steal the milkman from me? Admit it! Admit about the milkman. His youth and vigour excite you, don't they? Admit about the milkman. For Solange says: to hell with you!

CLAIRE: (*panic-stricken*). Claire! Claire!

SOLANGE: Eh?

CLAIRE: (*in a murmur*). Claire, Solange, Claire.

SOLANGE: Ah! Yes, Claire, Claire says: to hell with you! Claire is here, more dazzling than ever. Radiant! (*She slaps Claire.*)

CLAIRE: Oh! . . . Oh! Claire. . . . You. . . . Oh!

SOLANGE: Madame thought she was protected by her barricade of flowers, saved by some special destiny, by a sacrifice. But she reckoned without a maid's rebellion. Behold her wrath, Madame. She turns your pretty speeches to nought. She'll cut the ground from under your fine adventure. Your Monsieur was just a cheap thief, and you——

CLAIRE: I forbid you! Confound your impudence!

SOLANGE: Twaddle! She forbids me! It's Madame who's confounded. Her face is all convulsed. Would you like a mirror? Here. (*She hands Claire a mirror.*)

CLAIRE: (*regarding herself with satisfaction*). I see the marks of a slap, but now I'm more beautiful than ever!

SOLANGE: Yes, a slap!

CLAIRE: Danger is my halo, Claire; and you, you dwell in darkness. . . .

SOLANGE: But the darkness is dangerous.—I know. I've heard all that before. I can tell by your face what I'm supposed to answer. So I'll finish it up. Now, here are the two maids, the faithful servants! They're standing in front of you. Despise them. Look more beautiful. We no longer fear you. We're merged, enveloped in our fumes, in our revels, in our hatred of you. The mould is setting. We're taking shape, Madame. Don't laugh—ah! above all, don't laugh at my grandiloquence. . . .

CLAIRE: Get out!

SOLANGE: But only to be of further service to Madame! I'm going back to my kitchen, back to my gloves and the smell of my teeth. To my belching sink. You have your flowers, I my sink. I'm the maid. You, at least, you can't defile me. But! But! . . . (*She advances on Claire, threateningly.*) But before I go back, I'm going to finish the job. (*Suddenly an alarm clock goes off. Solange stops. The two actresses, in a state of agitation, run together. They huddle and listen.*) Already?

CLAIRE: Let's hurry! Madame'll be back. (*She starts to unfasten her dress.*) Help me. It's over already. And you didn't get to the end.

SOLANGE: (*helping her. In a sad tone of voice*). The same thing happens every time. And it's all your fault, you're never ready. I can't finish you off.

CLAIRE: We waste too much time with the preliminaries. But we've still. . . .

SOLANGE: (*as she helps Claire out of her dress*). Watch at the window.

CLAIRE: We've still got a little time left. I set the clock so we'd be able to put the things in order. (*She drops wearily into the armchair.*)

SOLANGE: (*gently*). It's so close this evening. It's been close all day.

CLAIRE: (*gently*). Yes.

SOLANGE: Is that what's killing us, Claire?

13

CLAIRE: Yes.

SOLANGE: It's time now.

CLAIRE: Yes. (*She gets up wearily.*) I'm going to make the tea.

SOLANGE: Watch at the window.

CLAIRE: There's time. (*She wipes her face.*)

SOLANGE: Still looking at yourself . . . Claire, dear. . . .

CLAIRE: Let me alone, I'm exhausted.

SOLANGE: (*sternly*). Watch at the window. Thanks to you, the whole place is in a mess again. And I've got to clean Madame's gown. (*She stares at her sister.*) Well, what's the matter with you? You can be like me now. Be yourself again. Come on, Claire, be my sister again.

CLAIRE: I'm finished. That light's killing me. Do you think the people opposite. . . .

SOLANGE: Who cares! You don't expect us to . . .(*she hesitates*) organize things in the dark? Have a rest. Shut your eyes. Shut your eyes, Claire.

CLAIRE: (*she puts on her short black dress*). Oh! When I say I'm exhausted, it's just a way of talking. Don't use it to pity me. Stop trying to dominate me.

SOLANGE: I've never tried to dominate you. I only want you to rest. You'll help me more by resting.

CLAIRE: I understand, don't explain.

SOLANGE: Yes, I will explain. It was you who started it. When you mentioned the milkman. You think I couldn't see what you were driving at? If Mario——

CLAIRE: Oh!

SOLANGE: If the milkman says indecent things to me, he does to you, too. But you loved mingling. . . .

CLAIRE: (*shrugging her shoulders*). You'd better see whether everything's in order. Look, the key of the secretary was like this (*she arranges the key*) and, as Monsieur says——

SOLANGE: (*violently*). You loved mingling your insults——

CLAIRE: He's always finding the maids' hairs all over the pinks and roses!

SOLANGE: And things about our private life with——

CLAIRE: With? With? With what? Say it! Go on, name it! The ceremony? Besides, we've no time to start a discussion

14

now. She'll be back, back, back! But, Solange, this time we've got her. I envy you; I wish I could have seen the expression on her face when she heard about her lover's arrest. For once in my life, I did a good job. You've got to admit it. If it weren't for me, if it hadn't been for my anonymous letter, you'd have missed a pretty sight: the lover handcuffed and Madame in tears. It's enough to kill her. This morning she could hardly stand up.

SOLANGE: Fine. She can drop dead! And I'll inherit! Not to have to set foot again in that filthy garret, with those two idiots, that cook and that butler.

CLAIRE: I really liked our garret.

SOLANGE: Just to contradict me. Don't start getting sentimental about it. I loathe it and I see it as it really is, bare and mean. And shabby. But what of it! We're just scum!

CLAIRE: Ah! No, don't start that again. Better watch at the window. I can't see a thing. It's too dark outside.

SOLANGE: Let me talk. Let me get it out of my system. I liked the garret because it was plain and I didn't have to put on a show. No hangings to push aside, no rugs to shake, no furniture to caress—with my eyes or with a rag, no mirrors, no balcony. Nothing forced us to make pretty gestures. Don't worry, you'll be able to go on playing queen, playing at Marie Antoinette, strolling about the apartment at night.

CLAIRE: You're mad! I've never strolled about the apartment.

SOLANGE: (*ironically*). Oh, no. Mademoiselle has never gone strolling! Wrapped in the curtains or the lace bedcover. Oh no! Looking at herself in the mirrors, strutting on the balcony at two in the morning, and greeting the populace which has turned out to parade beneath her windows. Never, oh no, never.

CLAIRE: But, Solange——

SOLANGE: It's too dark at night for spying on Madame, and you thought you were invisible on your balcony. What do you take me for? Don't try to tell me you walk in your sleep. At the stage we've reached you can admit it.

CLAIRE: But, Solange, you're shouting. Please, please lower your voice. Madame may come in without making a sound. . . . (*She runs to the window and lifts the curtain.*)

SOLANGE: All right, I've had my say. Let go of the curtains. Oh, I can't stand the way you lift them. Let go of them. It upsets me; that's how Monsieur did it when he was spying on the police, the morning he was arrested.

CLAIRE: So you're scared now? The slightest gesture makes you feel like a murderer trying to slip away by the service stairway.

SOLANGE: Go on, be sarcastic, work me up! Go on, be sarcastic! Nobody loves me! Nobody loves us!

CLAIRE: *She* does, *she* loves us. She's kind. Madame is kind! Madame adores us.

SOLANGE: She loves us the way she loves her armchair. Not even *that* much! Like her bidet, rather. Like her pink enamel lavatory seat. And we, we can't love one another. Filth. . . .

CLAIRE: Ah! . . .

SOLANGE: . . . doesn't love filth. D'you think I'm going to put up with it, that I'm going to keep playing this game and then at night go back to my folding-cot? The game! Will we even be able to go on with it? And if I have to stop spitting on someone who calls me Claire, I'll simply choke! My spurt of saliva is my spray of diamonds!

CLAIRE: (*she stands up and cries*). Speak more softly, please, please. Speak—speak of Madame's kindness.

SOLANGE: Her kindness, is it? It's easy to be kind, and smiling, and sweet—ah! that sweetness of hers!—when you're beautiful and rich. But what if you're only a maid? The best you can do is to give yourself airs while you're doing the cleaning or washing up. You twirl a feather duster like a fan. You make fancy gestures with the dishcloth. Or like *you*, you treat yourself to historical parades in Madame's apartment.

CLAIRE: Solange! You're starting again! What are you trying to do? We'll never calm down if you talk like that! I could say a thing or two about you.

SOLANGE: You? You?

CLAIRE: Yes, me. If I wanted to. Because, after all. . . .

SOLANGE: All? After all? What are you insinuating? It was you
who started talking about that man. Claire, I hate you.

CLAIRE: Same to you and more! But if I wanted to provoke you
I wouldn't have to use the milkman as an excuse. I've
got something better on you and you know it.

SOLANGE: Who's going to get the better of who? Eh? Well, say
something!

CLAIRE: Go on, start it! You hit first. It's you who're backing
out, Solange. You don't dare accuse me of the worst:
my letters. Pages and pages of them. The garret was
littered with them. I invented the most fantastic stories
and you used them for your own purposes. You
frittered away my frenzy. Yesterday, when you were
Madame, I could see how delighted you were at the
chance they gave you to stow away on the *Lamartinière*,
to flee France in the company of your lover——

SOLANGE: Claire——

CLAIRE: Your lover, to Devil's Island, to Guiana. You were
delighted that my letters allowed you to be the
prostitute kneeling at the feet of the thief. You were
happy to sacrifice yourself, to bear the cross of the
impenitent thief, to wipe his face, to stand by him, to
take his place in the galleys so that he could rest. And
you felt yourself growing. Your brow rose higher than
mine, it rose above the palm trees.

SOLANGE: But what about you, just before, when you were talking
about following him. . . .

CLAIRE: Right. I don't deny it. I took up where you left off.
But with less violence than you. Even in the garret,
amidst all the letters, you started swaying back and
forth with the pitching of the boat.

SOLANGE: You didn't see yourself——

CLAIRE: I did. I'm more sensible than you. You're the one who
concocted the story. Turn your head. Ha! If only you
could see yourself, Solange. Your face is still lit up by
the sun setting through the virgin forest! You're

17

planning his escape! (*She laughs nervously.*) You certainly do work yourself up! But don't let it worry you; it would be cruel to disturb your blissful voyage. I hate you for other reasons, and you know what they are.

SOLANGE: (*lowering her voice*). I'm not afraid of you. I know you hate me and that you're a sneak, but be careful now. I'm older than you.

CLAIRE: So what?—Older! And stronger too? You're trying to put me off by making me talk about that man. Hmph! You think I haven't found you out? You tried to kill her.

SOLANGE: Are you accusing me?

CLAIRE: Don't deny it. I saw you.
(*A long silence*).
And I was frightened. Frightened, Solange. Through her, it was me you were aiming at. I'm the one who's in danger. When we finish the ceremony, I'll protect my neck.
(*A long silence. Solange shrugs her shoulders.*)

SOLANGE: (*with decision*). Is that all? Yes, I did try. I wanted to free you. I couldn't bear it any longer. It made me suffocate to see you suffocating, to see you turning red and green, rotting away in that woman's bitter-sweetness. Blame me for it, you're right. I loved you too much. Had I killed her, you'd have been the first to denounce me. You'd have turned me over to the police, yes, you.

CLAIRE: (*she seizes her by the wrists*). Solange. . . .

SOLANGE: (*freeing herself*). What are *you* afraid of? It's *my* concern.

CLAIRE: Solange, my little sister, she'll be back soon.

SOLANGE: I didn't kill anyone. I was a coward, you realize. I did the best I could, but she turned over in her sleep. (*Rising exaltation.*) She was breathing softly. She swelled out the sheets: it was Madame.

CLAIRE: Stop it.

SOLANGE: Now you want to stop me. You wanted to know, didn't you? Well, wait, I've got some more to tell you. You'll

18

see what your sister's made of. What stuff she's made of. What a servant girl really is. I wanted to strangle her——

CLAIRE: Let me alone. Think of what comes after.

SOLANGE: Nothing comes after. I'm sick and tired of kneeling in pews. In church I'd have had the red velvet of abbesses or the stone of the penitents, but my bearing at least would have been noble. Look, just look at how she suffers. How she suffers in beauty. Grief transfigures her, doesn't it? Beautifies her? When she learned that her lover was a thief, she stood up to the police. She exulted. Now she is forlorn and splendid, supported under each arm by two devoted servants whose hearts bleed to see her grief. Did you see it? Her grief sparkling with the glint of her jewels, with the satin of her gowns, in the glow of the chandelier! Claire, I wanted to make up for the poverty of my grief by the splendour of my crime. Afterward, I'd have set fire to the lot.

CLAIRE: Solange, calm down. The fire might not have caught. You'd have been found out. You know what happens to incendiaries.

SOLANGE: I know everything. I kept my eye and ear to the keyhole. No servant ever listened at doors as I did. I know everything. Incendiary! It's a splendid title.

CLAIRE: Be quiet. I'm stifling. You're stifling me. (*She wants to open the window.*) Oh! Let's have some air!

SOLANGE: Get away from the window. Open the anteroom and the kitchen doors. (*Claire opens both doors.*) Go and see whether the water's boiling.

CLAIRE: All alone?

SOLANGE: Wait, all right, wait till she comes. She's bringing her stars, her tears, her smiles, her sighs. She'll corrupt us with her sweetness.

(*The telephone rings. The two sisters listen.*)

CLAIRE: (*at the telephone*). Monsieur? It's Monsieur! . . . This is Claire, Monsieur. . . . (*Solange wants to hear too, but Claire pushes her away.*) Very well. I'll inform Madame.

Madame will be overjoyed to hear that Monsieur is free. . . . Yes, Monsieur. . . . Very well. . . . Good-bye, Monsieur. (*She wants to hang up, but her hand trembles, and she lays the receiver on the table.*)

SOLANGE: Is he out?

CLAIRE: The judge let him out on bail.

SOLANGE: Well, you've done a fine job. My compliments. Your denunciations, your letters, it's working out beautifully. And if they recognize your handwriting, it'll be perfect.

CLAIRE: Please, please, don't overwhelm me. Since you're so clever, you should have managed your business with Madame. But you were afraid. The bed was warm. The air thick with perfume. It was Madame! We've got to carry on with the same kind of life. With the same old game. But, you poor wretch, even the game is dangerous. I'm sure we've left traces. We leave them every time. I see a host of traces I'll never be able to cover up. And she, she walks about in her tamed menagerie. She unravels the clues. She points to our traces with the tip of her pink toe. She discovers us, one by one. Madame jeers at us. And it's your fault. All's lost because you lacked strength.

SOLANGE: I can still find whatever strength I need.

CLAIRE: Where? Where? You've been outstripped by *me*. You don't live above the treetops. A milkman passing through your mind gets you all flustered.

SOLANGE: It was because I couldn't see her face, Claire. Because I was so close to Madame, so close to her sleep. I lost my strength. In order to get at her throat, I'd have had to lift the sheet from her heaving bosom.

CLAIRE: (*ironically*). And the sheets were warm. The night dark. That kind of thing has to be done in broad daylight. You're incapable of it. It's too terrible a deed. But *I* can manage it.

SOLANGE: Claire!

CLAIRE: Where you botched it, *I'll* succeed.

SOLANGE: (*she runs a comb through her hair*). Claire, don't get carried away, don't be rash——

CLAIRE: What makes you think I'm being rash? First of all, don't mix your hairpins up with mine! You . . . Oh! All right, mix your muck with mine. Mix it! Mix your rags with my tatters! Mix it all up. It'll stink of the maids. So Monsieur won't have any trouble discovering us. And we'll die in a flood of shame. (*Suddenly calm.*) I'm capable of anything, you know.

SOLANGE: The sleeping pills.

CLAIRE: Yes. Let's talk calmly. I'm strong. You tried to dominate me. . . .

SOLANGE: But, Claire——

CLAIRE: (*calmly*). I beg your pardon, but I know what I'm saying. I've made up my mind. I'm ready. I'm tired of it all. Tired of being the spider, the umbrella-case, the shabby, godless nun, without a family! I'm tired of having a stove for an altar. I'm that disagreeable, sullen, smelly girl. To you, too.

SOLANGE: Claire . . . we're both nervous. (*Anxiously*). Where's Madame? I can't stand it any more either. I can't stand our being so alike, I can't stand my hands, my black stockings, my hair. I'm not reproaching you for anything, my little sister. I understand that your strolls through the flat helped ease the strain.

CLAIRE: (*irritated*). Ah! Stop it!

SOLANGE: I want to help you. I want to comfort you, but I know I disgust you. I'm repulsive to you. And I know it because you disgust me. When slaves love one another, it's not love.

CLAIRE: And me, I'm sick of seeing my image thrown back at me by a mirror, like a bad smell. You're my bad smell. Well, I'm ready. Ready to bite. I'll have my crown and I shall stroll about the apartment.

SOLANGE: That's not reason enough to kill her.

CLAIRE: Really? Why, please? For what other reason? Where and when could we find a better excuse? Ah, so it's not enough, not enough to be raped by a milkman who goes blithely through our garrets? Tonight Madame will witness our shame. Bursting with laughter, laughing until the tears roll down her face, with her flabby sighs. No. I shall have my crown. I shall be the poisoner that you failed to be. It's my turn now to dominate you!

SOLANGE: But I never. . . .

CLAIRE: Hand me the towel! Hand me the clothes-pegs! Peel the onions! Scrape the carrots! Scrub the tiles! It's over. Over. Ah! I almost forgot! Turn off the tap! It's over. (*Exalted*) I'll run the world!

SOLANGE: My little baby sister!

CLAIRE: You'll help me.

SOLANGE: You won't know what gestures to make. Things are more serious, Claire, and simpler too.

CLAIRE: (*exalted*). We've read the story of Sister Holy Cross of the Blessed Valley who poisoned twenty-seven Arabs. She walked without shoes, with her feet all stiff. She was lifted up, carried off to the crime. We've read the story of Princess Albanarez who caused the death of her lover and her husband. She uncorked the bottle and made a big sign of the cross over the goblet. As she stood before the corpses, she saw only death and, off in the distance, the fleet image of herself being carried by the wind. She made all the gestures of earthly despair. In the book about the Marquise de Venosa, the one who poisoned her children, we're told that, as she approached the bed, her arms were supported by the ghost of her lover.

SOLANGE: Baby sister, my angel!

CLAIRE: I'll be supported by the sturdy arms of the milkman. I'll lean my left hand on the back of his neck. He won't flinch. You'll help me. And, far away, Solange, if we have to go far away, if I have to leave for Devil's Island, you'll come with me. You'll board the boat. The flight you were planning for him can be used for me. We shall be that eternal couple, Solange, the two of us, the eternal couple of the criminal and the saint. We'll be saved, Solange, saved, I swear to you! (*She falls on Madame's bed.*)

SOLANGE: Be calm. You're going to sleep. I'll carry you upstairs.

22

CLAIRE: Let me alone. Turn out the light. Please turn out the light. (*Solange turns out the light.*)

SOLANGE: Rest. Rest, little sister. (*She kneels, removes Claire's shoes, kisses her feet.*) Be calm, my darling. (*She caresses her.*) Put your feet on my shoulders. There. Close your eyes.

CLAIRE: (*she sighs*). I'm ashamed, Solange.

SOLANGE: (*very gently*). Don't talk. Leave things to me. I'm going to put you to bed and, when you fall asleep, I'll carry you upstairs, to the garret. I'll undress you and put you into your little cot. Sleep. I'll be here.

CLAIRE: I'm ashamed, Solange.

SOLANGE: Sh! Let me tell you a story.

CLAIRE: (*simply*). Solange.

SOLANGE: My angel?

CLAIRE: Solange, listen. . . .

SOLANGE: Sleep. (*A long silence.*)

CLAIRE: You have lovely hair. You have such lovely hair. Hers——

SOLANGE: Don't talk about her any more.

CLAIRE: Hers is false. (*A long silence.*) Do you remember? Under the tree, just the two of us? Our feet in the sun? Solange?

SOLANGE: I'm here. Sleep. I'm your big sister.
(*Silence. A moment later Claire gets up.*)

CLAIRE: No! No weakness! Put the light on! Put it on! Quick! It's too great a moment! (*Solange puts the light on.*) Stand up. And let's eat. What's in the kitchen? Eh? We've got to eat. To be strong. Come along, you'll advise me. The phenobarbital.

SOLANGE: I'm too exhausted. Yes, the phenobarbital.

CLAIRE: The phenobarbital! Don't make such a face. We must be joyous. And sing. Let's sing! Sing, the way you'll sing when you go begging in the courts and embassies! Laugh! (*They burst out laughing.*) Otherwise, it'll be so tragic that we'll go flying out of the window. Shut the window. (*Solange, laughing, shuts the window.*) Murder is a thing that's . . . unspeakable!

SOLANGE: Let's sing! We'll carry her off to the woods, and under the fir trees we'll cut her to bits by the light of the moon. And we'll sing. We'll bury her beneath the flowers, in our flower beds, and at night—we'll water her *toes* with a little *hose*! (*The front doorbell rings.*)

CLAIRE: It's Madame!

SOLANGE: It must be her! Straighten the bed. (*She seizes her sister by the wrists.*) Claire, are you sure you can go through with it?

CLAIRE: How many do we need?

SOLANGE: About ten. Put ten pills into her tea. Will you do it?

CLAIRE: (*she frees herself, goes to tidy the bed, stares at it for a moment.*) Yes. I've got the tube in my pocket.
(*Exit Solange, left. Claire continues tidying the room and leaves right. A few seconds elapse. A burst of nervous laughter backstage. Madame, in a fur coat, enters laughing with Solange behind her.*)

MADAME: There's no end to it! Such horrible gladioli, such a sickly pink, and mimosa! They probably hunt through the market before dawn to get them cheaper. (*Solange helps her off with her coat.*)

SOLANGE: Madame wasn't too cold?

MADAME: Yes, Solange, I was very cold. I've been trailing through corridors all night long. I've been seeing frozen men and stony faces, but I did manage to catch a glimpse of Monsieur. From a distance. I waved to him. I've only just left the wife of a magistrate. Claire!

SOLANGE: She's preparing Madame's tea.

MADAME: I wish she'd hurry. I'm ashamed to ask for tea when Monsieur is all alone, without a thing, without food, without cigarettes.

SOLANGE: But Monsieur won't stay there long. They'll see right away that he's not guilty.

MADAME: Guilty or not, I shall never desert him, never. You see, Solange, it's at times like this that you realize how much you love someone. I don't think he's guilty either, but if he were, I'd become his accomplice. I'd follow him to Devil's Island, to Siberia.

24

SOLANGE: There's no need to get panicky. I've seen worse cases acquitted. There was a trial in Bordeaux——

MADAME: Do you go to trials? You?

SOLANGE: I read the crime news. It was about a man who——

MADAME: You can't compare Monsieur's case. He's been accused of the most idiotic thefts. I know he'll get out of it. All I mean is that, as a result of this preposterous affair, I've come to realize how deeply attached I am to him. Of course, none of this is serious, but if it were, Solange, it would be a joy for me to bear his cross. I'd follow him from place to place, from prison to prison, on foot if need be, as far as the penal colony.

SOLANGE: They wouldn't let you. Only bandits' wives, or their sisters, or their mothers, are allowed to follow them.

MADAME: A condemned man is no longer a bandit. And then I'd force my way in, past the guards. (*Suddenly coquettish.*) And, Solange, I'd be utterly fearless. I'd use my weapons. What do you take me for?

SOLANGE: Madame mustn't get such ideas into her head. You must rest.

MADAME: I'm not tired. You treat me like an invalid. You're always ready to coddle me and pamper me as if I were dying. Thank God, I've got my wits about me, I'm ready for the fight. (*She looks at Solange and, feeling that she has hurt her, adds, with a smile*) Come, come, don't make such a face. (*With sudden violence*) All right, it's true! There are times when you're so sweet that I simply can't stand it. It crushes me, stifles me! And those flowers which are there for the very opposite of a celebration!

SOLANGE: If Madame means that we lack discretion. . . .

MADAME: But I didn't mean anything of the kind, my dear girl. It's just that I'm so upset. You see what a state I'm in.

SOLANGE: Would Madame like to see the day's accounts?

MADAME: You certainly picked the right time. You must be mad. Do you think I could look at figures now? Show them to me tomorrow.

SOLANGE: (*putting away the fur cape*). The lining's torn. I'll take it to the furrier tomorrow.

MADAME: If you like. Though it's hardly worth while. I'm giving up my wardrobe. Besides, I'm an old woman.

SOLANGE: There go those gloomy ideas again.

MADAME: I'm thinking of going into mourning. Don't be surprised if I do. How can I lead a worldly life when Monsieur is in prison? If you find the house too sad. . . .

SOLANGE: We'll never desert Madame.

MADAME: I know you won't, Solange. You've not been too unhappy with me, have you?

SOLANGE: Oh!

MADAME: When you needed anything, I saw that you got it. With my old gowns alone you both could have dressed like princesses. Besides . . .(*She goes to the closet and looks at her dresses*) of what use will they be to me? I'm through with finery and all that goes with it. (*Claire enters carrying the tea.*)

CLAIRE: The tea is ready.

MADAME: Farewell to parties and dances and the theatre. You'll inherit all that.

CLAIRE: Madame is losing her self-control. She must pull herself together.

SOLANGE: The tea is ready.

MADAME: Put it down. I'm going to bed. It's all over. (*She runs her hand over the red velvet dress.*) My lovely "Fascination", the loveliest of them all. (*She takes it down and runs her hand over it.*) It was designed for me by Chanel. Specially. Here, you may have it. It's yours. (*She gives it to Claire and searches in the closet.*)

CLAIRE: For me?

MADAME: (*smiling sadly*). Of course. I said so, didn't I?

SOLANGE: Madame is very kind. (*To Claire.*) You might thank Madame. You've been admiring it so long.

CLAIRE: It's so beautiful. I'll never dare wear it.

MADAME: You can have it altered. There's enough velvet in the train alone for the sleeves. And for you, Solange, I'm going to give you. . . . What shall I give you? Here, this coat. (*She hands Solange the magnificent fur cape.*)

CLAIRE: Oh! the fur cape!

SOLANGE: (*thrilled*). Oh! Madame . . . never . . . Madame's too kind.

MADAME: No, no, don't thank me. It's such a pleasure to make people happy. Now I'm going to get undressed. (*She looks at the telephone.*) Who left the receiver off?

CLAIRE: It was Monsieur. . . . (*She stops suddenly.*)

MADAME: (*dumbfounded*). Eh? Monsieur? (*Claire is silent.*) What do you mean? Speak up!

SOLANGE: (*slowly and as if in spite of herself*). When Monsieur rang up.

MADAME: What are you talking about? Monsieur phoned?

SOLANGE: We wanted to surprise Madame. Monsieur's out on bail. He's waiting for Madame at the Hong-Kong Bar.

MADAME: (*rising to her feet*). And you didn't say anything! Go get a taxi! Solange, quick, quick, get me a taxi. And hurry up. Go on, run. (*She pushes Solange out of the room.*) My furs! Quick, quick! You're both mad. You let me go on talking. You really are mad. Or am *I* going mad! (*She puts on her fur coat. To Claire.*) When did he phone?

CLAIRE: (*in a toneless voice*). Five minutes before Madame came in.

MADAME: But you should have told me. And this cold tea! I'll never be able to wait for Solange to get back! Oh! What did he say?

CLAIRE: What I've just told you. He was very calm.

MADAME: Ah, him, he always is. He'd be utterly unconcerned if he were condemned to death. The man's unique! What else did he say?

CLAIRE: Nothing. He said the judge was letting him out.

MADAME: How can anyone leave police headquarters at midnight? Do judges work as late as that?

CLAIRE: Sometimes much later.

MADAME: Much later? How do *you* know that?

CLAIRE: I read *True Detective*. I know those things.

27

MADAME: (*astonished*). Oh you do? You really are an odd little girl, Claire. She *might* hurry. (*She looks at her wrist watch.*) You won't forget to have the lining of my coat sewn?

CLAIRE: I'll take it to the furrier tomorrow. (*A long silence.*)

MADAME: What about the accounts? The day's accounts. Let me see them. I've got time!

CLAIRE: Solange attends to that.

MADAME: That's right. I'm all in a dither. I'll look at them tomorrow. (*Staring at Claire.*) Come a little closer! Come here! Why . . . you've got make-up on! (*Laughing*). Why, Claire, you've been putting make-up on!

CLAIRE: (*very embarrassed*). Madame. . . .

MADAME: Ah, don't lie! Besides, you've every right to. Live, my child, live. In whose honour is it? Eh? Got a crush on someone? Own up!

CLAIRE: I put a little powder on. . . .

MADAME: That's not powder, it's make-up. But there's nothing wrong in that, you're still young. Make yourself attractive. Smarten up. (*She puts a flower in Claire's hair. She looks at her wrist watch.*) What *can* she be doing? It's midnight and she's not back!

CLAIRE: There aren't many taxis at this hour. She probably had to run to the cab-stand.

MADAME: You think so? I've lost track of time. I'm wild with happiness. Monsieur ringing up at a time like that! And that he's free.

CLAIRE: Madame ought to sit down. I'll go and heat up the tea. (*She starts to leave.*)

MADAME: Don't bother, I'm not thirsty. It's champagne we'll be drinking tonight. You can be sure we won't be coming home.

CLAIRE: Really, just a little tea. . . . .

MADAME: (*laughing*). I'm nervous enough as it is. I don't want you and Solange to wait up for us. Go upstairs and get to bed right away. (*Suddenly she sees the alarm clock.*) But. . . . That alarm clock, what's that doing here? Where does it come from?

CLAIRE: (*very embarrassed*). The alarm clock? It's the kitchen clock.

MADAME: It is? I've never seen it before.

CLAIRE: (*she takes the alarm clock*). It belongs on the shelf. It's always been there.

MADAME: (*smiling*). It's true I'm something of a stranger in the kitchen. You're at home there. It's your domain. You're its sovereigns. But, I wonder why you brought it in here?

CLAIRE: It was Solange, for the cleaning. She'd never dare trust the big clock.

MADAME: How odd.

(*Claire goes out carrying the alarm clock.*)

How odd. (*She looks at her wrist watch.*) She's certainly taking her time. You can find taxis at every street-corner. (*She sits down at her dressing table. She looks at herself in the mirror and talks to herself.*) And what about you, you fool, will you be beautiful enough to receive him? No wrinkles, eh? It's been such a long separation, it'll have been like a thousand years! Eh? Let's see, now. Gay? Wistful? Idiot, you idiot, there I go talking to myself. Happiness makes me giddy. And Solange not back yet. All those flowers! Those girls do worship me, but—(*she looks at the top of the dressing table and blows at the powder*) but they haven't dusted the dressing table. Their housekeeping is the most extraordinary combination of luxury and filth.

(*As she utters the last sentence, Claire enters the room on tiptoe. She stands silent behind Madame who suddenly notices her in the mirror.*) Eh? I'm raving, Claire, my mind's wandering. Forgive me. Today's been too dreadful.

CLAIRE: Isn't Madame satisfied with our work?

MADAME: (*smiling*). But I am, Claire. Delighted. In seventh heaven.

CLAIRE: Madame's making fun of us.

MADAME: (*laughing*). Oh, stop nagging me. After what I've been through today, I've got a right to be out of sorts. In the first place, there's that business of the letters to the police. . . . I wonder who could have sent them. I suppose you wouldn't have any idea?

CLAIRE: Does Madame mean? . . .

MADAME: I don't mean anything. I'd like to know, that's all. I've been groping around the whole day long as if I were blind. I felt like the police hunting in the bushes for a girl's corpse.

CLAIRE: That's all over with. Monsieur is free.

MADAME: Thank heavens. Which still doesn't account for those letters. What *can* she be doing? She's been gone an hour. Why didn't you tell me at once that Monsieur had phoned? He'll be furious.

CLAIRE: We were terribly afraid of alarming Madame, of giving her a shock.

MADAME: That was very bright. You're quietly killing me with flowers and kindness. One fine day I'll be found dead beneath the roses. Claire, what do you think of this coiffure? Do you like it?

CLAIRE: If I might venture. . . .

MADAME: Eh? If you might venture? Well, venture. I've full confidence in your opinion. Well? What do you think of it?

CLAIRE: If I might be so bold as to make a suggestion, Madame's hair would look fluffier worn over the forehead.

MADAME: Are you sure?

CLAIRE: It would soften Madame's face.

MADAME: Like that? You're right. You *are* a bright girl, Claire. You know, Claire, I've always thought you had a great deal of taste and that you were meant for better things.

CLAIRE: I'm not complaining.

MADAME: No, no, I know. But after all, you *are* more sensitive than the others. I realize that it's not much fun living with them. Fortunately you're with your sister. You're a family. But with a bit of luck you——

CLAIRE: Oh! If I had wanted to!

MADAME: I don't doubt it! (*She listens*). Listen! (*She stands up*).

Listen! A car. It's her. Ah! (*She looks at herself again in the mirror.*)

CLAIRE: Madame should have some tea because of the cold.

MADAME: (*laughing*). You're trying to kill me with your tea and your flowers and your suggestions. You're too much for me, Claire. No. I've never felt so alive. Oh! And served in the best tea set, the *very best* set! Such pomp! Such elegance! (*She wants to leave, but Claire stands between her and the door.*)

CLAIRE: (*imploringly*). Madame *must* drink it. Otherwise. . . . (*Solange dashes in. She pushes her sister aside and turns to Madame.*)

MADAME: Well!

SOLANGE: (*surprised*). Ah! Madame's still here. I've looked everywhere. No one wanted to come as late as this!

MADAME: Did you get a taxi?

SOLANGE: It's here, Madame. It's downstairs, Madame.

MADAME: Let's hurry. So it's understood, you're to go upstairs and to bed. And tomorrow morning we'll just sleep and sleep and sleep. Claire, come and close the door behind me. And you're not to latch it.
(*She leaves, followed by Claire. Solange is left alone. Claire returns. The two sisters look at one another.*)

SOLANGE: (*ironically*). You certainly did a fine job. And you sneered at me.

CLAIRE: Don't. I tried so hard not to say it, but I just couldn't help myself.

SOLANGE: Didn't she drink it? (*Claire shakes her head "no."*) Obviously. It was to be expected.

CLAIRE: I'd have liked to see *you* in my place. (*She remains motionless for a moment and then starts walking towards the kitchen.*)

SOLANGE: Where are you going?

CLAIRE: (*without turning around and in a weary voice*). To sleep! (*She leaves.*)

SOLANGE: Claire! (*Silence.*) Claire! (*She goes to the door and calls her.*) Claire, I'm calling you.

CLAIRE: (*off stage*). Who cares?

31

SOLANGE: (*facing the door at the right*). Come here. Do you hear me? Come here.
(*Claire comes in untying her apron.*)

CLAIRE: (*very wearily*). What do you want? Is it my fault? The "tay"—as she says—was ready. I put in the pills. She wouldn't drink it!

SOLANGE: And so you think we're just going to sit here and shake? (*She stares hard at her sister.*) They'll both be back tomorrow, drunk probably and vicious, like conquerors. They'll know where the letters came from. They—I hate her. (*Claire shrugs her shoulders.*) Oh, I hate her! I loathe her. And you, you just stand there! Didn't you see how she sparkled? How disgustingly happy she was? *Her* joy feeds on *our* shame. Her carnation is the red of our shame. Her dress. . . . (*She kicks at the red velvet dress.*) It's the red of our shame. Her furs. . . . Ah! She took back her furs! And you just stand there! You don't scream. Are you dead?

CLAIRE: What do you want me to do? She got away from us. You came back too soon.

SOLANGE: She gets away and you just stand there!

CLAIRE: What do you want to do? Make a scene? Eh? (*She screams in the face of Solange, who remains motionless.*) You want to make a scene? Answer. Answer. Well, answer. We've got time. We've got all night.

SOLANGE: (*in a very calm tone*). Let's get on with it.

CLAIRE: What's the hurry? No, we'll take our time. Shall we? (*She unties her apron.*)

SOLANGE: Keep your apron on. It's your turn.

CLAIRE: No, that doesn't matter.

SOLANGE: It's my turn to be Madame.

CLAIRE: Take the apron.

SOLANGE: But, Claire. . . .

CLAIRE: (*simply*). I'm used to it. Here. (*She delicately hands the apron to Solange.*) Do you think I've really got too much rouge on?

SOLANGE: Rouge? Yes, there's some rouge left. . . . But you're not rouged. You're all made-up.

CLAIRE: That's what she said.

SOLANGE: That's all over. (*She grabs the apron.*) Forced to wear that! But I want to be a real maid. (*She ties the strings behind her back.*) Put out the light.

CLAIRE: (*timidly*). You. . . . You don't want us to . . . to organize things in the dark?

SOLANGE: Do as I say. (*She puts out the light. The room is in semi-darkness. The two sisters look at one another and speak, without moving.*)

CLAIRE: Oh! Let's wait a little while, Solange. Suppose she comes back? Madame might have forgotten something. At times like that one always forgets . . . one's bag, or money, or. . . .

SOLANGE: Naïve!

CLAIRE: (*muttering*). She left in such a hurry. It's a trap. Madame suspects something.

SOLANGE: (*shrugging her shoulders*). What? For instance?

CLAIRE: She's suspicious. We're being watched. . . .

SOLANGE: What of it? We're beyond that!

CLAIRE: (*she wants to gain time*). You're not listening to me, Solange. I assure you, I feel something, I feel it. Listen, we're being spied on. I'm sure she'll come back unexpectedly. She'll have forgotten her handkerchief. Or her gloves. (*Solange shrugs her shoulders.*) Or her compact, God knows what. But I feel there's something here, Solange—something in this room—that can record our gestures and play them back. Remember, Madame told us not to latch the front door. . . .

SOLANGE: You're raving.

CLAIRE: I'm not! No! Please, wait, please, it's so serious. Suppose she came back. . . .

SOLANGE: Too bad for her!

CLAIRE: You're growing terrible, Solange. You've got an answer for everything. At least. . . .

SOLANGE: What?

CLAIRE: (*timidly*). At least . . . suppose we said a prayer?

SOLANGE: Do you dare bring God. . . .

CLAIRE: But to the Holy. . . .

SOLANGE: Bring the *Mother* of God into the ceremony? Really, you've got more nerve than I thought. You've no shame.

CLAIRE: More softly, Solange, the walls are thin.

SOLANGE: (*less loudly*). You're going mad, Claire. It's God who's listening to us. We know that it's for Him that the last act is to be performed, but we mustn't forewarn Him. We'll play it to the hilt.

CLAIRE: Not so loud!

SOLANGE: The walls are His ears.

CLAIRE: Then I'll put on the white dress.

SOLANGE: If you like. It makes no difference. But hurry up! Let's drop the preliminaries and get on with it. We've long since stopped needing the twists and turns and the lies. Let's get right into the transformation. Hurry up! Hurry up! I can't stand the shame and humiliation any longer. Who cares if the world listens to us and smiles and shrugs its shoulders and says I'm crazy and envious! I'm quivering, I'm shuddering with pleasure. Claire, I'm going to whinny with joy!
(*During this speech, Claire has taken down the white dress and, hidden behind a screen, has put it on over her black dress whose black sleeves show.*)

CLAIRE: (*appearing, all in white, with an imperious voice*). Begin!

SOLANGE: (*ecstatically*). You're beautiful.

CLAIRE: Skip that. You said we're skipping the prelude. Start the insults.

SOLANGE: I'll never be able to. You dazzle me.

CLAIRE: I said the insults! Let them come, let them unfurl, let them drown me, for, as you well know, I loathe servants. A vile and odious breed, I loathe them. They're not of the human race. Servants ooze. They're a foul effluvium drifting through our rooms and hallways, seeping into us, entering our mouths, corrupting us. I vomit you!

SOLANGE: Go on. (*Silence. Claire coughs.*) Go on! I'm getting there, I'm getting there!

34

CLAIRE: I know they're necessary, just as gravediggers and scavengers and policemen are necessary. Nevertheless, they're a putrid lot.

SOLANGE: Go on, go on!

CLAIRE: Your frightened guilty faces, your puckered elbows, your outmoded clothes, your wasted bodies, only fit for our castoffs! You're our distorting mirrors, our loathsome vent, our shame, our drags!

SOLANGE: Go on, go on!

CLAIRE: Please hurry. Please! I can't go on. You're . . . you're. . . . My God, I can't think of anything. My mind's a blank. I've run out of insults. Claire, you exhaust me.

SOLANGE: Stop. I've got there. It's my turn.—Madame had her billing and cooing, her lovers, her milkman. . . .

CLAIRE: Solange. . . .

SOLANGE: Silence! Her morning milkman, her messenger of dawn, her handsome clarion, her pale and charming lover. That's over. (*She takes down a riding whip.*) Take your place for the ball.

CLAIRE: What are you doing?

SOLANGE: (*solemnly*). I'm checking the flow. Down on your knees!

CLAIRE: Solange. . . .

SOLANGE: Down on your knees! (*Claire hesitates and kneels.*) Ah! Ah! You were so beautiful, the way you wrung your precious arms! Your tears, your petals oozed down your lovely face. Ah! Ah! Down! (*Claire does not move.*) Down! (*Solange strikes her.*) Get down! (*Claire lies down.*) Ah! You amuse me, my dear! Crawl! Crawl, I say, like a worm! And you were going to follow in the wake of the boats, to cross the sea to aid and comfort your handsome exile! Look at yourself again! That role is only for the fairest of the fair. The guards would snicker. People would point at you. Your lover would hang his head in shame! And are you strong enough? Strong enough to carry his bag? And spry enough, Madame, spry enough on your feet? Don't worry. I'm not jealous. I don't need that thief where I'm going. No, Madame. I myself am both the thief and his

35

slavish shadow. I move alone towards the brightest
shores.

CLAIRE: I'm losing him!

SOLANGE: Aren't I enough for you?

CLAIRE: Solange, please, I'm sinking.

SOLANGE: Sink! But rise again to the surface. I know what my
final destiny is to be. I've reached shelter. I can be
bountiful. (*She takes a breath.*) Stand up! I'll marry
you standing up! Ah! Ah! Grovelling on the rug at a
man's feet. What a sorry, facile gesture. The great
thing is to end in beauty. How are you going to get
up?

CLAIRE: (*getting up slowly and clumsily*). You're killing me.

SOLANGE: (*ironically*). Careful now, watch your movements.

CLAIRE: (*on her feet*). We're out of our depth. We must go to
bed. My throat's——

SOLANGE: (*striding up to her*). Madame has a very lovely throat.
The throat of a queen. (*Claire moves back to the kitchen
door.*) Of a dove. Come, my turtle dove!

CLAIRE (*she withdraws farther back, putting her hands to her
neck as if to protect it*). It's late.

SOLANGE: Never too late.

CLAIRE: Madame. . . .

SOLANGE: . . . . is drinking champagne with Monsieur who has
returned from the dead.

CLAIRE: She'll be back any moment. Let me go.

SOLANGE: Stop worrying. She's waltzing! She's waltzing! She's
guzzling fine wine! She's delirious.

CLAIRE: Let's get out of here, Solange. I tell you we're in
danger.

SOLANGE: Go into the vestry. (*She points to the kitchen door.*) Go
on in. You've got to finish the linoleum.

CLAIRE: (*she screams in a hollow voice*). Help!

SOLANGE: Don't yell! It's useless. Death is present, and is stalking
you. Don't yell! I, who kept you the way they keep
kittens for drowning. I, yes I, who trimmed my belly
with pins to stab all the foetuses I threw into the
gutter! In order to keep you, to have *you* alive!

36

CLAIRE: (*running about the room*). Solange, Solange, come to yourself!

SOLANGE: (*running after her*). To *your*self!

CLAIRE: (*in a dull voice*). Help!

SOLANGE: Stop yelling! No one can hear you! We're both beyond the pale.

CLAIRE: Solange. . . .

SOLANGE: Everyone's listening, but no one will hear.

CLAIRE: I'm ill. . . .

SOLANGE: You'll be taken care of there.

CLAIRE: I'm ill . . . I . . . I'm going to be sick. . . . (*She seems to be gagging.*)

SOLANGE: (*she approaches her and says sympathetically*). Really? Are you really ill? Claire, are you really feeling ill?

CLAIRE: I'm, I'm going to——

SOLANGE: Not here, Claire, hold it in. (*She supports her.*) Not here, please, please. Come. Lean on me. There. Walk gently. We'll be better off there, in our flowered domain. I have such sure ways of putting an end to all suffering.

(*They leave by the kitchen door. The stage remains empty for a few seconds. A gust of wind opens the unlocked window. Enter Solange, right, wearing her short black dress. Throughout the scene she will seem to be addressing characters who are imaginary, though present.*)

SOLANGE: Madame. . . . At last! Madame is dead! . . . laid out on the linoleum . . . strangled by the dish-gloves. What? Oh, Madame may remain seated. . . . Madame may call me Mademoiselle Solange. . . . Exactly. It's because of what I've done. Madame and Monsieur will call me Mademoiselle Solange Lemercier. . . . Madame should have taken off that black dress. It's grotesque. (*She imitates Madame's voice.*) So I'm reduced to wearing mourning for my maid. As I left the cemetery all the servants of the neighbourhood marched past me as if I were a member of the family. I've so often been part of the family. Death will see the joke through to the bitter end. . . . What? Oh! Madame needn't feel sorry for me.

37

I'm Madame's equal and I hold my head high. . . .
Oh! And there are things Monsieur doesn't realize. He
doesn't know that he used to obey our orders. (*She
laughs.*) Ah! Ah! Monsieur was a tiny little boy.
Monsieur toed the line when we threatened. No,
Inspector, no. . . . I won't talk! I won't say a word. I
refuse to speak about our complicity in this murder.
. . . . The dresses? Oh, Madame could have kept them.
My sister and I had our own. Those we used to put on
at night, in secret. Now, I have my own dress, and I'm
your equal. I wear the red garb of criminals.
Monsieur's laughing at me? He's smiling at me.
Monsieur thinks I'm mad. He's thinking maids should
have better taste than to make gestures reserved for
Madame! Monsieur really forgives me? Monsieur is the
soul of kindness. He'd like to vie with me in grandeur.
But I've scaled the fiercest heights. Madame now sees
my loneliness—at last! Yes, I am alone. And fearsome.
I might say cruel things, but I can be kind. . . .
Madame will get over her fright. She'll get over it well
enough. What with her flowers and perfumes and
gowns and jewels and lovers. As for me, I've my sister.
. . . Yes. I dare speak of these things. I do, Madame.
There's nothing I won't dare. And who could silence
me, who? Who would be so bold as to say to me: "My
dear child!" I've been a servant. Well and good. I've
made the gestures a servant must make. I've smiled at
Madame. I've bent down to make the bed, bent down
to scrub the tiles, bent down to peel vegetables, to
listen at doors, to glue my eye to keyholes! But now I
stand upright. And firm. I'm the strangler.
Mademoiselle Solange, the one who strangled her
sister! . . . Me be still? Madame is delicate, really. But
I pity Madame. I pity Madame's whiteness, her satiny
skin, and her little ears, and little wrists. . . . Eh? I'm
the black crow. . . . Oh! Oh! I have my judges. I
belong to the police. Claire? She was really very fond
of Madame. . . . YOUR dresses again! And THAT

white dress, THAT one, which I forbade her to put
on, the one you wore the night of the Opera Ball, the
night you poked fun at her, because she was sitting in
the kitchen admiring a photo of Gary Cooper. . . .
Madame will remember. Madame will remember her
gentle irony, the maternal grace with which she took
the magazine from us, and smiled. Nor will Madame
forget that she called her Clarinette. Monsieur laughed
until the tears rolled down his cheeks. . . . Eh? Who
am I? The monstrous soul of servantdom! . . . No,
Inspector, I'll explain nothing in their presence. That's
our business. It would be a fine thing if masters could
pierce the shadows where servants live. . . . That, my
child, is our darkness, ours. (*She lights a cigarette, and
smokes clumsily. The smoke makes her cough.*) Neither
you nor anyone else will be told anything. Just tell
yourselves that this time Solange has gone through
with it. . . . You see her dressed in red. She is going
out. (*She goes to the window, opens it, and steps out on
the balcony. Facing the night, with her back to the
audience, she delivers the following speech. A slight
breeze makes the curtains stir.*) Going out. Descending
the great stairway. Accompanied by the police. Out on
your balconies to see her making her way among the
shadowy penitents! It's noon. She's carrying a nine-
pound torch. The hangman follows close behind. He's
whispering sweet nothings in her ear. Claire! The
hangman's by my side! Now take your hand off my
waist. He's trying to kiss me! Let go of me! Ah! Ah!
(*She laughs.*) The hangman's trifling with me. She will
be led in procession by all the maids of the
neighbourhood, by all the servants who accompanied
Claire to her final resting place. They'll all be wearing
crowns, flowers, streamers, banners. They'll toll the
bell. The funeral will unfold its pomp. It's beautiful,
isn't it? First come the butlers, in full livery, but
without silk lining. They're wearing their crowns. Then
come the footmen, the lackeys in knee breeches and

white stockings. They're wearing their crowns. Then come the valets, and then the chambermaids wearing our colours. Then the porters. And then come the delegations from heaven. And I'm leading them. The hangman's lulling me. I'm being acclaimed. I'm pale and I'm about to die. . . . (*She returns to the room.*) And what flowers! They gave her such a lovely funeral, didn't they? Oh! Claire, poor little Claire! (*She bursts into tears and collapses into an armchair.*) What? (*She gets up.*) It's no use, Madame, I'm obeying the police. They're the only ones who understand me. They too belong to the world of outcasts, the world you touch only with tongs.

(*Visible only to the audience, Claire, during the last few moments, has been leaning with her elbows against the jamb of the kitchen door and listening to her sister.*)

Now we are Mademoiselle Solange Lemercier, that Lemercier woman. The famous criminal. And above all, Monsieur need not be uneasy. I'm not a maid. I have a noble soul. . . . (*She shrugs her shoulders.*) No, no, not another word, my dear fellow. Ah, Madame's not forgetting what I've done for her. . . . No, no, she must not forget my devotion. . . .

(*Meanwhile Claire enters through the door at the left. She is wearing the white dress.*)

And in spite of my forbidding it, Madame continues to stroll about the apartment. She will please sit down . . . and listen to me. . . . (*To Claire.*) Claire . . . we're raving!

CLAIRE: (*complainingly, Madame's voice*). You're talking far too much, my child. Far too much. Shut the window. (*Solange shuts the window.*) Draw the curtains. Very good, Claire!

SOLANGE: It's late. Everyone's in bed. . . . We're playing an idiotic game.

CLAIRE: (*she signals with her hand for silence*). Claire, pour me a cup of tea.

SOLANGE: But. . . .

40

CLAIRE: I said a cup of tea.

SOLANGE: We're dead-tired. We've got to stop. (*She sits down in an armchair.*)

CLAIRE: Ah, by no means! Poor servant girl, you think you'll get out of it as easily as that? It would be too simple to conspire with the wind, to make the night one's accomplice. Solange, you will contain me within you. Now pay close attention.

SOLANGE: Claire. . . .

CLAIRE: Do as I tell you. I'm going to help you. I've decided to take the lead. Your role is to keep me from backing out, nothing more.

SOLANGE: What more do you want? We're at the end. . . .

CLAIRE: We're at the very beginning.

SOLANGE: They'll be coming. . . .

CLAIRE: Forget about them. We're alone in the world. Nothing exists but the altar where one of the two maids is about to immolate herself——

SOLANGE: But——

CLAIRE: Be still. It will be your task, yours alone, to keep us both alive. You must be very strong. In prison no one will know that I'm with you, secretly. On the sly.

SOLANGE: I'll never be able. . . .

CLAIRE: Please, stand up straight. Up straight, Solange! Claire! Darling, stand straight now. Up straight. Pull yourself together.

SOLANGE: You're overwhelming me.

CLAIRE: A staff! A standard! Claire, up straight! I call upon you to represent me——

SOLANGE: I've been working too hard. I'm exhausted.

CLAIRE: To represent me in the world. (*She tries to lift her sister and keep her on her feet.*) My darling, stand up straight.

SOLANGE: Please, I beg of you.

CLAIRE: (*domineeringly*). I beg of you, stand up straight. Solemnly, Claire! Pretty does it, pretty does it! Up Claire! Up on your paws! (*She holds her by the wrists*

41

and lifts her from her chair.) Up on your paws! Now then! Up! Up!

SOLANGE: You don't realize the danger——

CLAIRE: But, Solange, you're immortal! Repeat after me——

SOLANGE: Talk. But not so loud.

CLAIRE: (*mechanically*). Madame must have her tea.

SOLANGE: (*firmly*). No, I won't.

CLAIRE: (*holding her by the wrists*). You bitch! Repeat. Madame must have her tea.

SOLANGE: I've just been through such a lot. . . .

CLAIRE: (*more firmly*). Madame will have her tea. . . .

SOLANGE: Madame will have her tea. . . .

CLAIRE: Because she must sleep. . . .

SOLANGE: Because she must sleep. . . .

CLAIRE: And I must stay awake.

SOLANGE: And I must stay awake.

CLAIRE: (*she lies down on Madame's bed*). Don't interrupt again. I repeat. Are you listening? Are you obeying? (*Solange nods "yes."*) I repeat: My tea!

SOLANGE: (*hesitating*). But. . . .

CLAIRE: I say: my tea.

SOLANGE: But, Madame.

CLAIRE: Good. Continue.

SOLANGE: But, Madame, it's cold.

CLAIRE: I'll drink it anyway. Let me have it. (*Solange brings the tray.*) And you've poured it into the best, the finest tea set. (*She takes the cup and drinks, while Solange, facing the audience, delivers the end of her speech.*)

SOLANGE: The orchestra is playing brilliantly. The attendant is raising the red velvet curtain. He bows. Madame is descending the stairs. Her furs brush against the green plants. Madame steps into the car. Monsieur is whispering sweet nothings in her ear. She would like to smile, but she is dead. She rings the bell. The porter yawns. He opens the door. Madame goes up the stairs. She enters her flat—but, Madame is dead. Her two maids are alive: they've just risen up, free, from Madame's icy form. All the maids were present

42

at her side—not they themselves, but rather the hellish agony of their names. And all that remains of them to float about Madame's airy corpse is the delicate perfume of the holy maidens which they were in secret. We are beautiful, joyous, drunk, and free!

CURTAIN